© **DAILY DOSE OF POSITIVE QUOTES**
BY SANDEEP RAVIDUTT SHARMA

Table of Contents

Introduction IV

Daily Dose of Positive Quotes...............................1

© DAILY DOSE OF POSITIVE QUOTES
BY SANDEEP RAVIDUTT SHARMA

Introduction

This book provides you with a **list of 100 motivational quotes and thoughts** focussing mainly on improving your wellness quotient. Living in the fast-paced world has its own set of advantages and disadvantages. On one hand it seems that with the modern gadgets, innovations, automation, life has become easy, but on the other hand, it is adding stress and putting pressure on the human mind. People are suffering from anxiety or depression due to modern lifestyle. Be ready to reinforce positivity every day. Train your mind to think positive and discard negative thoughts immediately. This book is just an attempt to present positive quotes for you. I'm sure if you keep reading, referring, sharing these thoughts and quotes, you may derive inspiration and develop a good understanding of various perspectives and facts about life..

"Take the daily dose of positivity to live a healthy life."

I sincerely hope, you will find this book amazing, interesting, rejuvenating, unique and constant source of inspiration.

Thank You and Happy Reading.

© DAILY DOSE OF POSITIVE QUOTES
BY SANDEEP RAVIDUTT SHARMA

© Copyright 2018 Sandeep Ravidutt Sharma - All rights reserved.

In no way is it legal to reproduce, duplicate, or transmit any part of this document in either electronic means or in printed format. Recording of this publication is strictly prohibited and any storage of this document is not allowed unless with written permission from the publisher. All rights reserved. The information provided herein is stated to be truthful and consistent, in that any liability, in terms of inattention or otherwise, by any usage or abuse of any policies, processes, or directions contained within is the solitary and utter responsibility of the recipient reader. Under no circumstances will any legal responsibility or blame be held against the author / publisher for any reparation, damages, or monetary loss due to the information herein, either directly or indirectly. The author own all copyrights.

Legal Notice:
This book is copyright protected. This is only for personal use. You cannot amend, distribute, sell, use, quote or paraphrase any part or the content within this book without the consent of the author or copyright owner. Legal action will be pursued if this is breached.

Disclaimer Notice:
Please note the information contained within this book is for motivational, educational and knowledge sharing purpose only. Every attempt has been made to provide the reader accurate, up to date and reliable complete information. No warranties of any kind are expressed or implied. Readers acknowledge that the author is not engaging in the rendering of legal, financial, medical or professional advice. By reading this document, the reader agrees that under no circumstances the author / publisher is responsible for any losses, direct or indirect, which are incurred as a result of the use of information contained within this document, including, but not limited to, —errors, omissions, or inaccuracies.

If you have further questions, contact on
Tel: +919969256731
Email: sandeepraviduttsharma@gmail.com

© **DAILY DOSE OF POSITIVE QUOTES**
BY SANDEEP RAVIDUTT SHARMA

Dedication

This book is dedicated to **Goddess Bhairavi**. In the Hindu religion, the Goddess Bhairavi represents divine anger and wrath which is directed towards impurities within us as well as to the negative forces that obstructs our spiritual growth. Bhairavi Mata is also called as **Shubhamkari** and does good things. She is often depicted in images as holding a book, rosary and making abhaya and varada mudra with her hands. She is fiercely protective, lending us wisdom and power, steadiness and clarity. She personifies light and fire, supporting us to reveal what we keep hidden and inviting us to explore our hidden mind and any secret darkness.

I hereby recite the following Bhairavi mool mantra...
"Om Hreem Bhairavi Kalaum Hreem Svaha"
And pray to **Goddess Bhairavi** for lending wisdom and power, steadiness and clarity in the life of my readers and the world. May Goddess Bhairavi protect us from negative forces along with removing impurities of our mind.

DAILY DOSE OF POSITIVE QUOTES

© **DAILY DOSE OF POSITIVE QUOTES**
BY SANDEEP RAVIDUTT SHARMA

You can freeze a golden moment in a photo frame but living a moment is one time and preferable to creating memories.

Each of us by birth is a stranger to the other. All relationships are formed after we start talking, liking and appreciating each other. Communication is the key to forging relationship.

© **DAILY DOSE OF POSITIVE QUOTES**
BY SANDEEP RAVIDUTT SHARMA

Those who understand you without uttering a single word are your real friends. Long live friendship.

You can't change your past but very well change your future.

© **DAILY DOSE OF POSITIVE QUOTES**
BY SANDEEP RAVIDUTT SHARMA

Running away from problems doesn't help anyone. It weakens your character and credibility.

Scaling Everest sounds good but returning back to the ground is natural.

You can attract positive energy by staying focused on what you want in life rather than allowing your attention of getting diverted to 'n' of goals and objectives.

The soul seeks peace and joy.

Larger roles await those who are thinking and doing big.

Motivation doesn't come to you on its own unless you are seeking it.

Differences in the relationship remain because we generally limit ourselves to our understanding of things from the way it looks from our end.

Be a friend in place of a distant relative. Share your pain and joy alike.

You should embark on your life journey even if no one is ready to join. It's better than just planning or talking about your journey.

A great leader becomes powerful not just by his position but by empowering the other.

Make others feel important and see how their approach towards you changes.

If you can't do much in sharing the pain and sufferings of others. At least refrain from adding more to it. Your kind words would be good enough to provide the healing touch.

Sharing your experiences with like-minded people makes you richer.

Ambitions are good when it makes you work and reach your destination.

© **DAILY DOSE OF POSITIVE QUOTES**
BY SANDEEP RAVIDUTT SHARMA

One disturbed mind can disturb the world. Put the, 'Do Not Disturb' sign on your mind by staying calm.

Get ready to burn your past if it is depressing.

© **DAILY DOSE OF POSITIVE QUOTES**
BY SANDEEP RAVIDUTT SHARMA

Opportunity simply walks in when the door is open. Don't close the doors unless you want the opportunity to knock and wait.

Addiction to anything is bad in the long term. Awareness of addiction can help you to decouple yourself in time.

© **DAILY DOSE OF POSITIVE QUOTES**
BY SANDEEP RAVIDUTT SHARMA

Get up if you are still in the sleeping mode. The break should not become the destination. The journey of life doesn't end in a day or two. Keep Going.

Sometimes Mist is all around in your life and you lose direction. Remember no Mist is forever, stand still for some time and the path would be clear again.

© **DAILY DOSE OF POSITIVE QUOTES**
BY SANDEEP RAVIDUTT SHARMA

Your knowledge, attitude and behaviour can make you Smart and not just by buying the smart gadget.

Good habits take time to settle down. You need to work hard with consistency and disciple to cultivate good habits.

You can negotiate only when the other person is interested. First check out the interest level and then move forward.

Be passionate about whatever you do. That's the mantra of achieving success.

© **DAILY DOSE OF POSITIVE QUOTES**
BY SANDEEP RAVIDUTT SHARMA

Be in touch with people you know who are close to your heart. You automatically get a morale booster with positivity full on.

Celebrating the accomplishments act as a motivator for the next triumph.

Your real wealth is your goodwill and credibility in the mind of the other and not just your money.

Instead of talking and reaching the deadline, let's call it a frontline that matters.

Behave the way you are. Don't pretend to know all. Express what you feel and don't care for the world. Believe in yourself. Follow rules but break them when you see yourself becoming the slave to it. Enjoy the freedom of expression and lend your voice not just for you but for the world. Positive and negative thoughts are two sides of the same coin. Extremes of both culminate into the other. So be normal and do what your heart says.

One can't wish rightly on an empty stomach. Once the basic needs are in place, one can think and aim big in life.

© **DAILY DOSE OF POSITIVE QUOTES**
BY SANDEEP RAVIDUTT SHARMA

Attempt to understand life but don't get stuck in the process. Life is beautiful and clarity would emerge soon.

You can recover loss of money but not your hard earned reputation. Live up to your reputation whether you win or lose in life.

You just can't win a war in absence of motivation and leadership. Clear understanding and acceptance of the purpose instilled by the leader are the first step forward followed by motivation and execution of good thought out plan.

Dreams give you the sight of your goalpost but no one can score the goal for you.

If you are keen to hate. Hate the hatred within you. Love will automatically come out due to lack of space.

Thoughts are immortal and come back to you in varied forms and in different lives. So beware of the impact, train your mind and heart towards giving birth to positive and actionable thoughts.

Seriousness can be useful when you are trying to understand the other person's perspective. When you don seriousness, it may also make you a good listener. It makes the other person comfortable to share intricate details with you. Be serious to understand the other and not for life.

Become a sword to protect innocent lives and not to kill them.

Trust helps to build and connect fast. Forget about trusting others. Even if you start by trusting your own abilities, you can win.

Don't accept failure without trying.

When you are on the side of truth and honesty the fear ends.

Whether you carry joy or sorrow in your life entirely depends on your mindset. How you treat your current situation makes you feel pain or happiness.

Burn the flag of darkness with the fire of knowledge, positive thinking and attitude.

Thank God for providing you with food, clothing and shelter. There are many others who can't even win daily bread. Show kindness by feeding the needy.

Hats off to those who share their meal with the hungry before taking their first bite.

Smash the issues before they force you to look into the trash.

Get rid of fear by riding on the horse of courage.

Laughter buries all your worries. If you can't laugh with others, at least laugh alone.

You can play and win any game of life if you have a good appetite for failure as well.

The fountain of happiness goes up and down in life. It depends on you how much you retain in your mind forever.

Get rid of the attachment if you want to live happily.

You can't hide the glow of happiness for long. Your face and behaviour reveals it all.

© **DAILY DOSE OF POSITIVE QUOTES**
BY SANDEEP RAVIDUTT SHARMA

Freedom outweighs every other benefit.

Avoid thinking too much about the failure, find time in honing and perfecting your skills to win next time.

© **DAILY DOSE OF POSITIVE QUOTES**
BY SANDEEP RAVIDUTT SHARMA

Time invites you to accompany in the journey of joy and togetherness. Those who like to walk slow often miss out while joy chooses some other partner.

Your choice of the path decides your success.

© **DAILY DOSE OF POSITIVE QUOTES**
BY SANDEEP RAVIDUTT SHARMA

The season of love and happiness is always there for you. It all depends on whether you want to still look for it wearing dark glasses or accept it with an open heart in the current form and be happy.

Habits stick to you unless you are consistently making attempt to get rid of them.

The moment someone speaks words like, 'Get out', a chain of events based on hatred is created. The end result is always detrimental for all concerned. Try to avoid such phrases by following a peaceful path wherein it's a win-win situation for both and the aim is also achieved. Rude behaviour always invites regret and repentance at a future date. Choose your words wisely.

When you frequently break the promises made, you weave in black and white a cobweb of mistrust. After this even if you try to convince using various means, people won't trust you. Build Trust... Don't Break It.

Replace the grudge with forgiveness, and you will feel good and lighter.

The journey of life is pleasant for those who have mastered the art of enjoying every moment.

© **DAILY DOSE OF POSITIVE QUOTES**
BY SANDEEP RAVIDUTT SHARMA

If you do something different then you are sure to get different results from the usual one.

Builders of man-made structures promise you various amenities and luxurious lifestyle facilities at a steep cost. Still, all these cannot match with what Mother Nature provides for her child living in a small cottage. Be grateful to mother nature and fellow humans who are striving hard to maintain the beautiful look of this wonderful planet.

Self-belief is better than listening to false praise.

Sky has got a big heart and is ready to accommodate many. Blue Sky appears to be pleasant and cool. Become a Sky and win over the world.

Time is never right or wrong. It's your mind which decides it. Keep the positive frame of mind.

Nothing comes for free in this world which man has created.

Time honours your presence or at other times disown you completely.

When you dance, don't bother about the world but focus on your own steps.

© DAILY DOSE OF POSITIVE QUOTES
BY SANDEEP RAVIDUTT SHARMA

Have you ever seen Flowers fight with each other? Forget about the flowers even thorns are not interested to fight.

If you have still got time and not the money, you can bounce back in life.

© **DAILY DOSE OF POSITIVE QUOTES**
BY SANDEEP RAVIDUTT SHARMA

The bicycle of life cannot run on its own. Efforts and choice of the direction are all yours.

Arrest your fall further by holding the virtues of discipline and positive attitude.

Rose and Thorns: Rose depicts life and thorn stands for pain. Rose without thorns is not complete. In the same way life without joy and sorrow is no life at all. Nobody wants to embrace thorns depicting sorrow. You don't have a choice as both joy and sorrow are twins born to Live.

You ignore the world, and everyone starts talking about you. You keep seeking the attention of the world, and the world makes you invisible. The best thing to do is keep sharing good things in life and maintain balance in your approach. Too much of anything is too bad including extreme positivity or negativity.

You can't fake sincerity. It reveals itself.

When opportunity comes your way and due to some reason you have missed it. Don't lose heart, the next big opportunity is close to your door and is about to knock. Be ready to grab it this time.

Focus on the cloud of positivity and you can ignore the dark and gloomy nature of mankind.

You won't find yourself even if you look hundred times in a mirror. Because it's only your heart which can see and knows the soul... Or who are you.

The positive thinker hardly knows anything about failure. He knows either Success or Lessons.

When you are not able to do anything and feel helpless. Leave it to time. Time heals every wound and resolves all kind of issues.

Don't just accept the modern ways of life as it comes, pay more attention to whether modernity is providing any qualitative benefits to you. If not then stick to the tested ways of life recommended by our ancestors. The best would be a balanced approach wherein you get the best of the old and modern world.

When you checked into this world, people could hear your cry but they laughed and celebrated. When you check out of this world, ensure that with your kindness and cheerful attitude, you had the last laugh and people still crave to hear it again and again when you depart.

The balance sheet of Life always tallies. Breath you earned = breath you have spent. Life = Breath in - Breath out. Breath in your aspiration, efforts, joy and breath out your failures, pain and hopelessness.

The time in your watch may or may not match with others. But your enthusiasm to expedite your assignment would surely rub on to others positively.

Set the alarm only when you really intend to wake up and go. Don't set it when you are used to giving excuses.

Beautiful memories refresh your mind and inspire to live.

Burning desire to succeed helps one to wake up in time and pursue the goals in time. With sincere and innovative efforts, nothing is impossible for the positive thinker.

Divinity can only be felt if you have the purity of thoughts. With complete devotion and love, you can find the Lord.

Hold the power of positivity always. Be ready to share the positive vibes and make this world a better place to live in.

You can't stop Time just by tying the hands of the clock. Keep pace with time if you really want to leave your mark on this world.

Trust the Lord, and your prayers will be answered. Pray for the well being of the other and asking for additional strength to face life challenges.

Working to earn your living is fine but doing it for helping others to learn and work is the best.

God gives you what you ask with a pure mind and good intentions.

In the fast moving world still the smile is the easiest and quickest way to transfer your best wishes. Keep smiling.

www.ingramcontent.com/pod-product-compliance
Lightning Source LLC
Chambersburg PA
CBHW070803220526
45466CB00002B/521